You've Totally GOT This!

You've Totally GOT This!

FRANCES MACLEOD

GIBBS SMITH
TO ENRICH AND INSPIRE HUMANKIND

NEW BEGINNINGS ARE often disguised AS PAINFUL ENDINGS.

THERE ARE

far better things ahead

THAN ANY
WE LEAVE BEHIND.

C.S. LEWIS

the secret of getting AHEAD is getting STARTED.

great people
do things
BEFORE
they're ready.

Amy Poehler

YOU GET IN
LIFE
OPRAH WINFREY
WHAT YOU HAVE
COURAGE
to ASK FOR.

YOU DON'T HAVE TO SEE THE WHOLE STAIRCASE, JUST TAKE THE FIRST STEP.

DOCTOR MARTIN LUTHER KING JR.

YOU CAN, YOU SHOULD,
AND IF YOU'RE
BRAVE ENOUGH
TO START,
YOU WILL.

STEPHEN KING

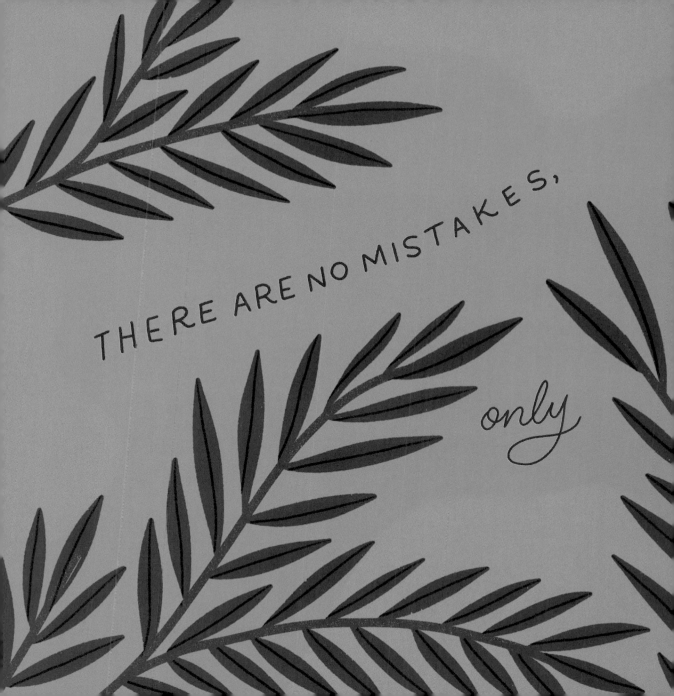

THERE ARE NO MISTAKES,

only

OPPORTUNITIES.

TINA FEY

a ship
is always safe
at shore,
but that's not
what a ship
is built for.

DOUBT
KILLS MORE
dreams
THAN
FAILURE
EVER WILL.

suzy kassem

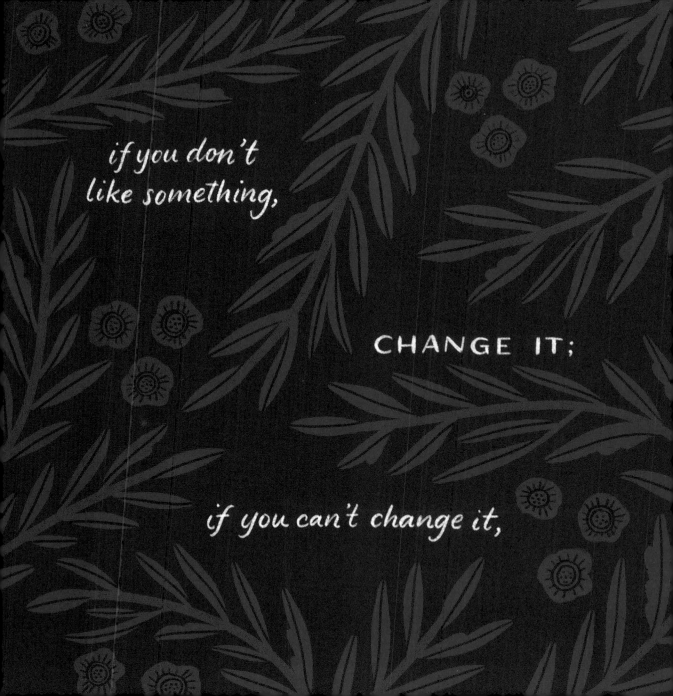

*if you don't
like something,*

CHANGE IT;

if you can't change it,

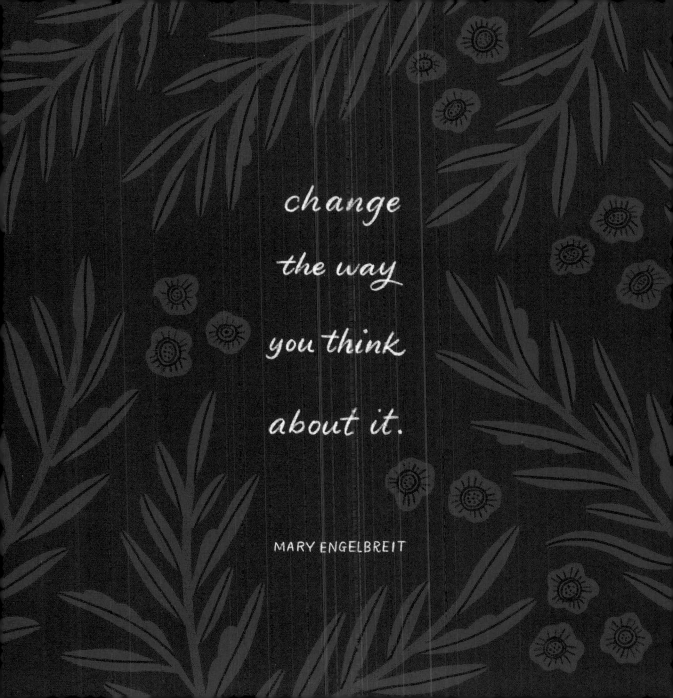

change

the way

you think

about it.

MARY ENGELBREIT

DON'T BE AFRAID TO GIVE UP THE GOOD AND GO FOR THE GREAT.

A PERSON WHO NEVER MADE A MISTAKE NEVER TRIED ANYTHING NEW.

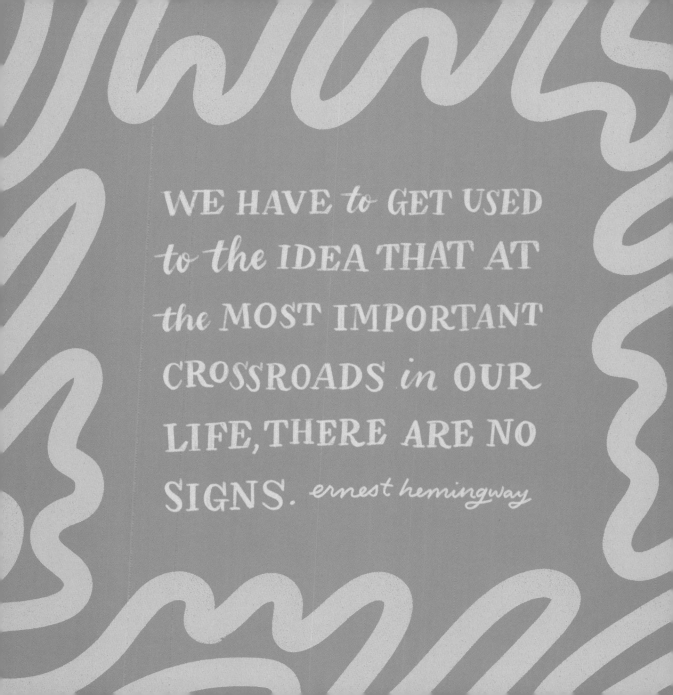

WE HAVE *to* GET USED *to the* IDEA THAT AT *the* MOST IMPORTANT CROSSROADS *in* OUR LIFE, THERE ARE NO SIGNS. *ernest hemingway*

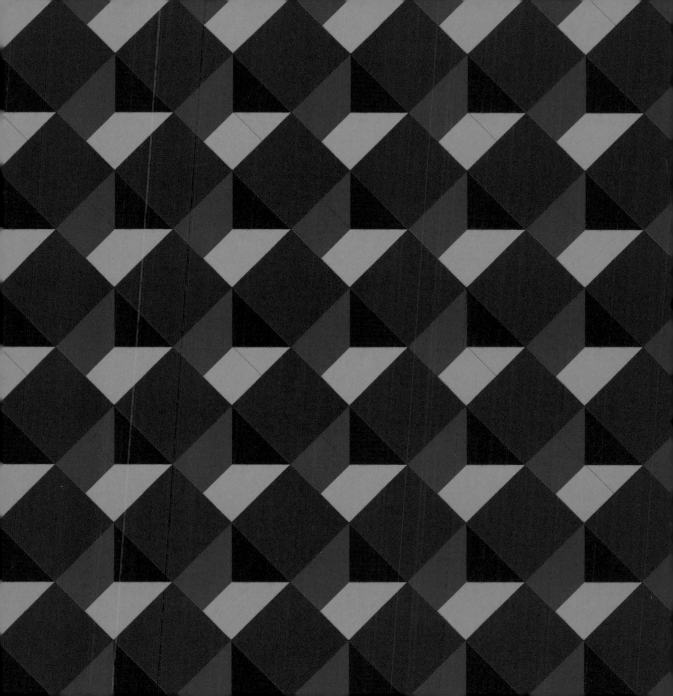

IT IS NEVER TOO LATE TO BE WHO YOU MIGHT HAVE BEEN.

WE MUST DO
THAT WHICH
WE THINK WE
CANNOT. ELEANOR
ROOSEVELT

THE BIGGEST design project anyone can have is THEIR OWN LIFE.

JESSI ARRINGTON

OPPORTUNITY
IS MISSED BY
PEOPLE BECAUSE IT
is DRESSED
IN OVERALLS
& LOOKS LIKE
WORK.

LIFE IS TOUGH

my darling

BUT SO ARE YOU.

STEPHANIE BENNET-HENRY

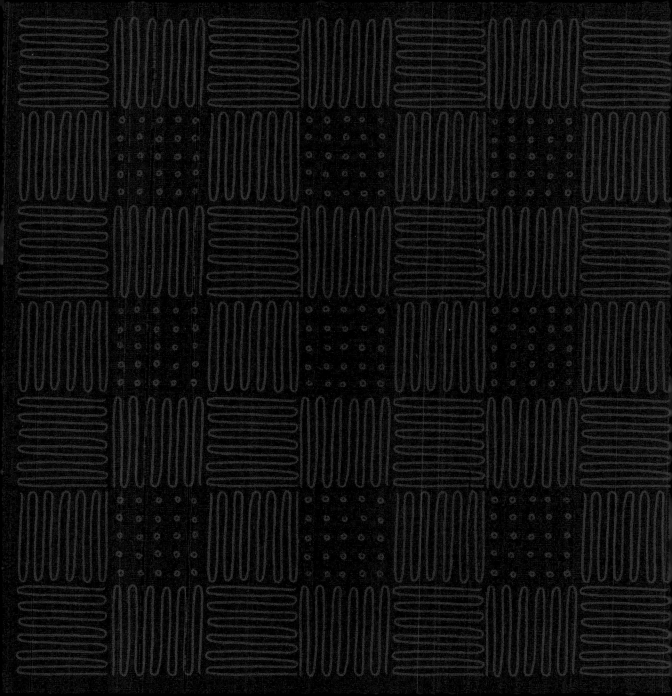

whether you think YOU CAN or YOU CAN'T, you're right.

REAL
GENEROSITY
TOWARD THE
FUTURE
LIES IN
GIVING ALL
TO THE
PRESENT.

ALBERT CAMUS

I am not *a* PRODUCT *of my* CIRCUMSTANCES.

I AM A PRODUCT *of* MY *DECISIONS.*

STEPHEN COVEY

Failure
IS THE
OPPORTUNITY
— TO —
Begin Again
MORE INTELLIGENTLY.

— HENRY FORD —

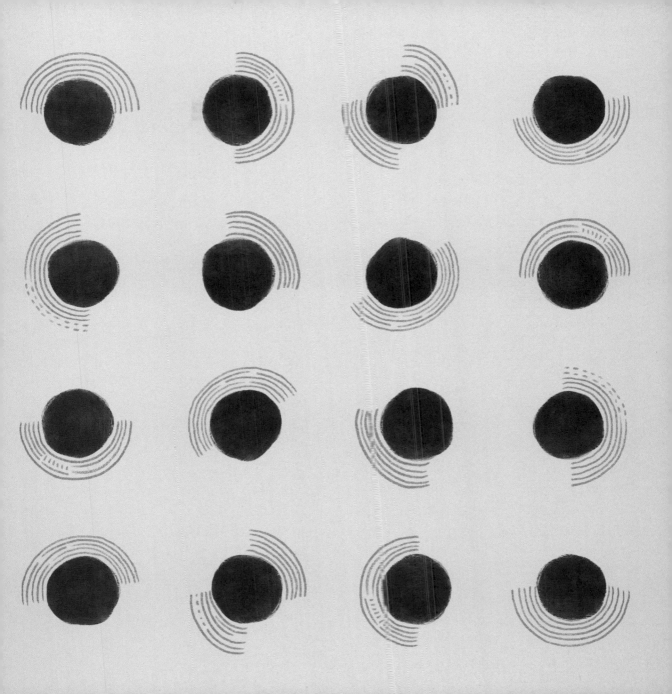

I DON'T WANT OTHER PEOPLE to DECIDE WHO I AM.

I WANT TO DECIDE THAT for MYSELF.

EMMA WATSON

Persistence
HAS ITS OWN
Momentum.

CHERYL STRAYED

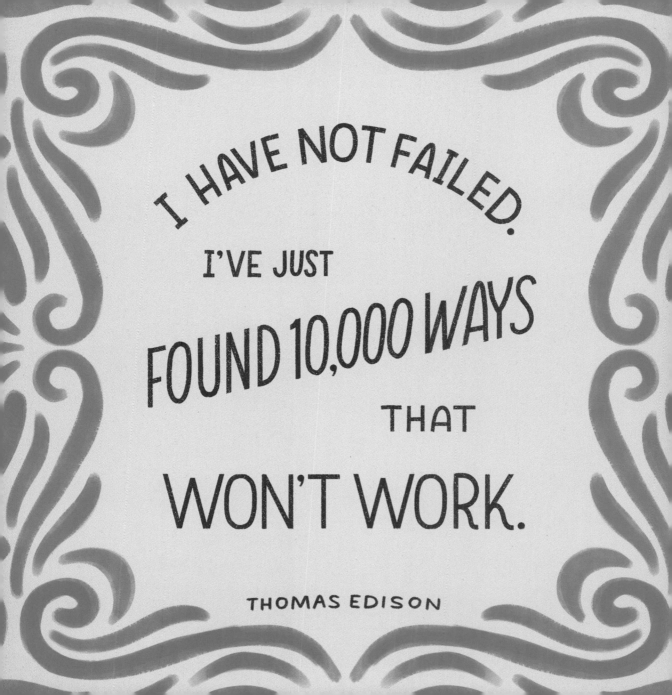

I HAVE NOT FAILED. I'VE JUST FOUND 10,000 WAYS THAT WON'T WORK.

THOMAS EDISON

LIFE *has* MANY WAYS
of TESTING
A PERSON'S WILL

EITHER by HAVING NOTHING HAPPEN
———— *at all* ————

OR BY HAVING EVERYTHING ——HAPPEN—— ALL AT ONCE.

paulo coelho

IT ALWAYS SEEMS
impossible
UNTIL IT IS
DONE

DON'T COMPARE YOUR BEGINNING to

SOMEONE ELSE'S MIDDLE.

TIM HILLER

ALMOST EVERYTHING
WILL WORK AGAIN
IF YOU
UNPLUG IT *for*
A FEW MINUTES,

anne lamott

INCLUDING YOU.

What is
creative living?
Any life
that is driven
more strongly
by curiosity
than fear.

ELIZABETH
GILBERT

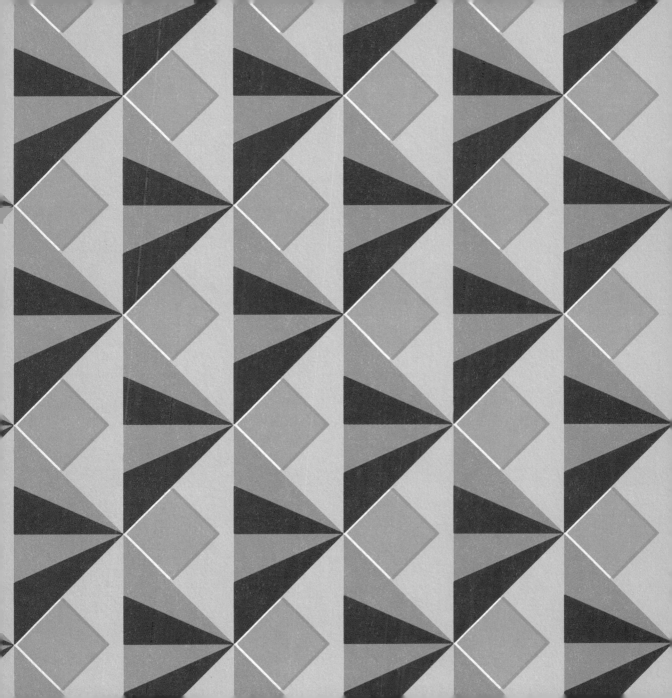

DO WHAT YOU HAVE TO DO UNTIL YOU CAN DO WHAT YOU WANT TO DO.

OPRAH.

My entire life
can be described
in one sentence:
It didn't go as
planned and
that's okay.

Rachel Wolchin

JUST SAY YES

and you'll figure it out afterwards. TINA FEY

WE
delight
IN THE
BEAUTY
of the
BUTTERFLY

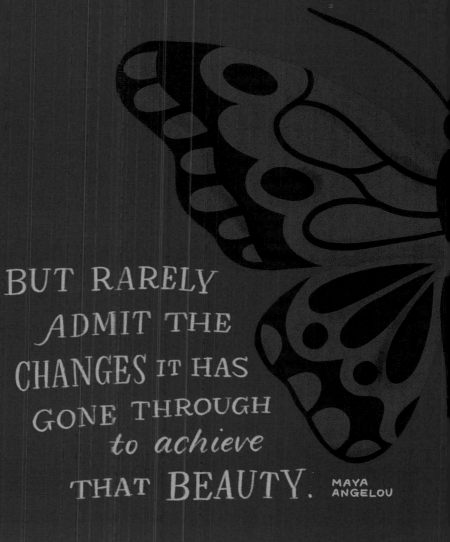

BUT RARELY
ADMIT THE
CHANGES IT HAS
GONE THROUGH
to achieve
THAT BEAUTY. MAYA
ANGELOU

THERE ARE *seven days* IN A WEEK.

eleanor roosevelt

WE GAIN STRENGTH, AND
COURAGE, *and* CONFIDENCE

BY EACH EXPERIENCE
IN WHICH WE REALLY STOP

to LOOK
FEAR IN THE FACE.

NO MATTER WHAT
PEOPLE TELL YOU

WORDS
& IDEAS
— can —
CHANGE THE
WORLD.

dead poets society

we can choose
COURAGE
or we can choose
comfort,
but we can't have both.
Not at the same time.

BRENÉ BROWN

SUCCESS IS NOT *FINAL* FAILURE IS NOT *FATAL*

IT IS THE
COURAGE
to CONTINUE
THAT **COUNTS.**

YOU CAN DO
anything,

JUST NOT
everything.

WHEN THE RIGHT PATH

REVEALS ITSELF,

FOLLOW IT.

CHERYL STRAYED

SUCCESS

— IS —

LIKING YOURSELF,
LIKING WHAT YOU DO,

— AND —

LIKING HOW YOU DO IT.

MAYA ANGELOU

THINGS TAKE
THE TIME
THEY TAKE.

don't worry.

MARY OLIVER,
"DON'T WORRY"

If you're too COMFORTABLE, it's time to move on. TERRIFIED of what's next? You're on the RIGHT TRACK.

SUSAN FALES-HILL

IT'S KIND of FUN TO DO the IMPOSSIBLE.

WALT DISNEY

be led

by your dreams.

Ralph Waldo Emerson

NEVER GIVE UP
ON A
DREAM
EARL NIGHTINGALE
BECAUSE *of* THE
TIME IT WILL TAKE to
ACCOMPLISH IT.
THE TIME WILL PASS
—— *anyway.* ——

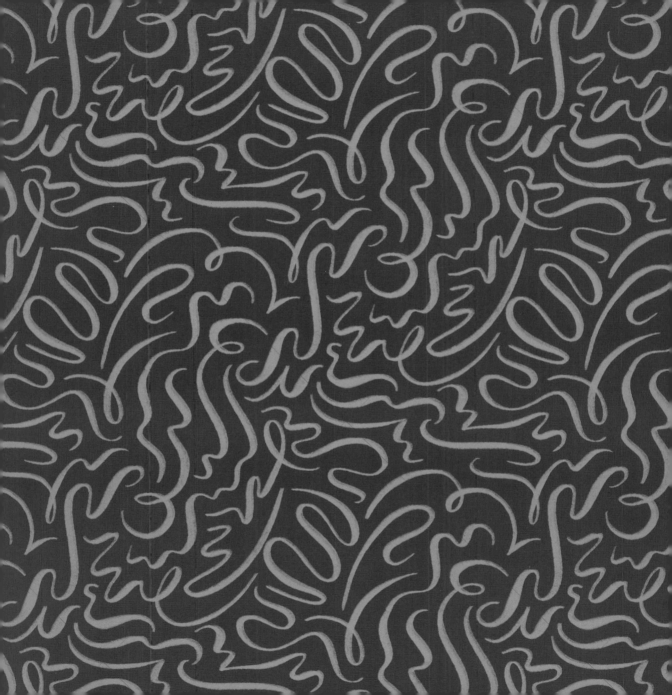

SUCCESS DOESN'T COME FROM WHAT YOU DO OCCASIONALLY, IT COMES FROM WHAT YOU DO CONSISTENTLY.

maria forleo

you can't wait for
INSPIRATION.

you have to
go after it
with a club.

JACK LONDON

and I NEVER QUIT TRYING.

—DOLLY PARTON

Whether you succeed or not is irrelevant—there is no such thing.

Making your
unknown known
is the important
thing — and keeping
the unknown always
beyond you.

Georgia O'Keeffe

keep some room
IN YOUR HEART
for the
UNIMAGINABLE.

mary oliver,
"*evidence*"

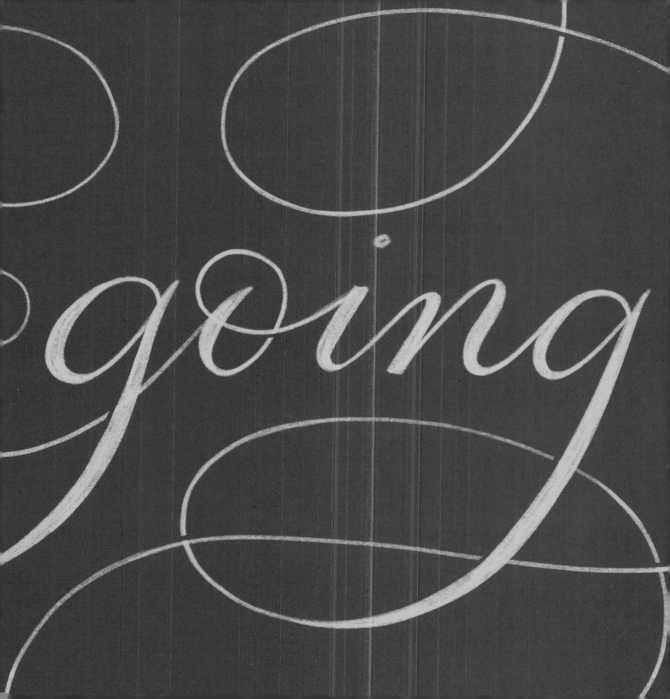

FRANCES MACLEOD
IS A BROOKLYN-BASED LETTERING
ARTIST AND ILLUSTRATOR. AN ALUMNA
OF COLUMBIA COLLEGE CHICAGO AND TYPE@
COOPER, SHE HAS WORKED IN CHICAGO AND
NEW YORK WITH CLIENTS SUCH AS KRAFT,
MCDONALD'S, AND FACEBOOK. FIND HER
ON INSTAGRAM: @FRANCESBLANK.

23 22 21 20 19   5 4 3 2

Published by
Gibbs Smith
P.O. Box 667
Layton, Utah 84041

1.800.835.4993 orders
www.gibbs-smith.com

Gibbs Smith books are printed on paper produced from
sustainable PEFC-certified forest/controlled wood source.
Learn more at www.pefc.org.

Printed and bound in China

Library of Congress Control Number: 2018951228
ISBN: 978-1-4236-5121-5